MW01280055

Positive Thinking:

365 Day Positive Thinking Journal:

Bring positive thinking into your life

365 Day Positive Thinking Journal

ISBN-13: 978-1530618323

ISBN-10: 1530618320

Give feedback on the book at:
me@jennykellett.com

Printed in U.S.A

Introduction

Thank you for purchasing this book. In my life, positive thinking has had a huge impact on my motivation and happiness. A few simple words can completely change your mindset from being negative and damaging to inspired and happy.

In this positive thinking journal I have hand-picked some of my favorite quotes that help inspire positive thinking. Each day, I encourage you to write down something that you loved about that day. It could be as simple as: 'I loved spending time with my family' or you can turn a negative experience into something positive, such as: 'I had a very disappointing day today BUT I learned from the experience'.

Of course, how you use this book is up to you, but I hope it will transform the way you think and give you the motivation to succeed.

Having a bad day? You can look back on previous journal entries and remind yourself that something good happens every day!

My favorite quotes...

Use this page to write down your favorite positive quotes

DATE : ....

WHAT I LOVED ABOUT TODAY:

"YOU SIMPLY HAVE TO PUT ONE FOOT IN
FRONT OF THE OTHER TO KEEP GOING. PUT
BLINDERS ON AND PLOW RIGHT AHEAD"

DATE : ....

WHAT I LOVED ABOUT TODAY:

"IF YOU DON'T DESIGN YOUR OWN LIFE PLAN, CHANCES ARE YOU'LL FALL INTO SOMEONE ELSE'S PLAN. AND GUESS WHAT THEY HAVE PLANNED FOR YOU? NOT MUCH."

DATE : ....

WHAT I LOVED ABOUT TODAY:

"DON'T JUDGE EACH DAY BY THE HARVEST YOU
REAP, BUT BY THE SEEDS YOU PLANT."

WHAT I LOVED ABOUT TODAY:

"OUR GREATEST WEAKNESS LIES IN GIVING UP. THE MOST CERTAIN WAY TO SUCCEED IS ALWAYS TO TRY JUST ONE MORE TIME."

DATE : ....

WHAT I LOVED ABOUT TODAY:

"NOTHING IS IMPOSSIBLE: THE WORD ITSELF
SAYS "I'M POSSIBLE""

WHAT I LOVED ABOUT TODAY:

"YOU ARE NEVER TOO OLD TO SET A NEW
GOAL OR DREAM ANOTHER DREAM."

DATE : ....

WHAT I LOVED ABOUT TODAY:

"EVERYONE WANTS TO LIVE AT THE TOP OF THE MOUNTAIN, BUT ALL THE HAPPINESS AND GROWTH OCCURS WHILE YOU'RE CLIMBING IT."

WHAT I LOVED ABOUT TODAY:

"THE BEST WAY TO GET SOMETHING DONE IS TO BEGIN."

DATE : ....

WHAT I LOVED ABOUT TODAY:

"AFTER A STORM COMES A CALM."

WHAT I LOVED ABOUT TODAY:

"A YEAR FROM NOW YOU MAY WISH YOU HAD STARTED TODAY."

DATE : ....

WHAT I LOVED ABOUT TODAY:

"YOU WERE BORN TO WIN, BUT TO BE A WINNER, YOU MUST PLAN TO WIN, PREPARE TO WIN, AND EXPECT TO WIN."

WHAT I LOVED ABOUT TODAY:

> "IF AND WHEN WERE PLANTED, AND NOTHING GREW."

DATE : ....

WHAT I LOVED ABOUT TODAY:

"THE TRAGEDY OF LIFE DOESN'T LIE IN NOT REACHING YOUR GOAL. THE TRAGEDY LIES IN HAVING NO GOAL TO REACH."

WHAT I LOVED ABOUT TODAY:

"DO IT NOW. SOMETIMES 'LATER BECOMES NEVER."

DATE : ....

WHAT I LOVED ABOUT TODAY:

"TRY NOT TO BECOME A MAN OF SUCCESS,
BUT A MAN OF VALUE."

WHAT I LOVED ABOUT TODAY:

"AS SOON AS YOU REALLY COMMIT TO MAKING SOMETHING HAPPEN, THE 'HOW' WILL REVEAL ITSELF."

DATE : ....

WHAT I LOVED ABOUT TODAY:

"EXPECT PROBLEMS AND EAT THEM FOR BREAKFAST."

WHAT I LOVED ABOUT TODAY:

"DON'T BELIEVE YOU HAVE TO BE BETTER THAN EVERYBODY ELSE. I BELIEVE YOU HAVE TO BE BETTER THAN YOU EVER THOUGHT YOU COULD BE."

DATE : ....

WHAT I LOVED ABOUT TODAY:

"DEAR TOMORROW, DO WHATEVER YOU WANNA DO... I HAVE ALREADY LIVED MY TODAY AND I AM NOT AFRAID OF YOU ANYMORE."

WHAT I LOVED ABOUT TODAY:

"PEOPLE WHO ARE CRAZY ENOUGH TO THINK THEY CAN CHANGE THE WORLD, ARE THE ONES WHO DO."

DATE : ....

WHAT I LOVED ABOUT TODAY:

"ENERGY FLOWS WHERE ATTENTION GOES."

WHAT I LOVED ABOUT TODAY:

"MAKE YOUR LIFE A MISSION — NOT AN INTERMISSION."

DATE : ....

WHAT I LOVED ABOUT TODAY:

"FALLING DOWN IS HOW WE GROW. STAYING DOWN IS HOW WE DIE."

WHAT I LOVED ABOUT TODAY:

"EVEN IF YOU FALL ON YOUR FACE, YOU'RE STILL MOVING FORWARD."

DATE : ....

WHAT I LOVED ABOUT TODAY:

"YOU CAN'T CROSS THE SEA MERELY BY STANDING AND STARING AT THE WATER."

WHAT I LOVED ABOUT TODAY:

"SUCCESS IS NOT FINAL, FAILURE IS NOT FATAL: IT IS THE COURAGE TO CONTINUE THAT COUNTS."

DATE : ....

WHAT I LOVED ABOUT TODAY:

"A RIVER CUTS THROUGH A ROCK NOT BECAUSE OF ITS POWER, BUT ITS PERSISTENCE."

WHAT I LOVED ABOUT TODAY:

"IF YOU CAN'T STOP THINKING ABOUT IT,
DON'T STOP WORKING FOR IT."

DATE : ....

WHAT I LOVED ABOUT TODAY:

"THE BEST WAY TO PREDICT THE FUTURE IS TO CREATE IT."

WHAT I LOVED ABOUT TODAY:

"WHEN YOU FEEL LIKE QUITTING, THINK ABOUT WHY YOU STARTED."

DATE : ....

WHAT I LOVED ABOUT TODAY:

"DON'T STOP WHEN YOU ARE TIRED. STOP WHEN YOU ARE DONE."

WHAT I LOVED ABOUT TODAY:

"I BELIEVE IN THE PERSON I WANT TO BECOME."

DATE : ....

WHAT I LOVED ABOUT TODAY:

"WAKE UP WITH DETERMINATION. GO TO BED WITH SATISFACTION."

WHAT I LOVED ABOUT TODAY:

"IN ORDER TO SUCCEED, WE MUST FIRST BELIEVE THAT WE CAN."

DATE : ....

WHAT I LOVED ABOUT TODAY:

"IF PLAN A DIDN'T WORK, THE ALPHABET HAS 25 MORE LETTERS."

WHAT I LOVED ABOUT TODAY:

"MISTAKES ARE PROOF THAT YOU ARE TRYING."

DATE : ....

WHAT I LOVED ABOUT TODAY:

"NOTHING WORTH HAVING COMES EASY."

WHAT I LOVED ABOUT TODAY:

"WORK UNTIL YOUR IDOLS BECOME YOUR RIVALS."

DATE : ....

WHAT I LOVED ABOUT TODAY:

"YOU ONLY FAIL WHEN YOU STOP TRYING."

44

WHAT I LOVED ABOUT TODAY:

"BE STUBBORN ABOUT YOUR GOALS, AND FLEXIBLE ABOUT YOUR METHOD."

DATE : ....

WHAT I LOVED ABOUT TODAY:

"DO SOMETHING TODAY THAT YOUR FUTURE SELF WILL THANK YOU FOR."

DATE : ....

WHAT I LOVED ABOUT TODAY:

"DON'T COUNT THE DAYS, MAKE THE DAYS COUNT."

DATE : ....

WHAT I LOVED ABOUT TODAY:

"YOUR ONLY LIMIT IS YOU."

DATE : ....

WHAT I LOVED ABOUT TODAY:

> "THERE IS NO ELEVATOR TO SUCCESS. YOU HAVE TO TAKE THE STAIRS."

DATE : ....

WHAT I LOVED ABOUT TODAY:

"SOMETIMES YOU WIN; SOMETIMES YOU LEARN."

WHAT I LOVED ABOUT TODAY:

"BELIEVING IN YOURSELF IS THE FIRST SECRET TO SUCCESS."

DATE : ....

WHAT I LOVED ABOUT TODAY:

"MAKE TODAY SO AWESOME THAT
TOMORROW GETS JEALOUS."

WHAT I LOVED ABOUT TODAY:

"IF YOU'RE GOING THROUGH HELL, KEEP GOING."

DATE : ....

WHAT I LOVED ABOUT TODAY:

"PUSH YOURSELF, BECAUSE NO ONE
ELSE IS GOING TO DO IT FOR YOU."

WHAT I LOVED ABOUT TODAY:

"STOP BEING AFRAID OF WHAT COULD GO WRONG AND START BEING POSITIVE ABOUT WHAT COULD GO RIGHT."

DATE : ....

WHAT I LOVED ABOUT TODAY:

"WITHOUT HARD WORK NOTHING GROWS BUT WEEDS."

WHAT I LOVED ABOUT TODAY:

"STRIVE FOR PROGRESS, NOT PERFECTION."

DATE : ....

WHAT I LOVED ABOUT TODAY:

> "FALL SEVEN TIMES; STAND UP EIGHT."

WHAT I LOVED ABOUT TODAY:

"SUCCESS ALL DEPENDS ON THE SECOND LETTER."

DATE : ....

WHAT I LOVED ABOUT TODAY:

"LIFE IS 10 PER CENT WHAT HAPPENS TO YOU, AND 90 PER CENT HOW YOU REACT."

WHAT I LOVED ABOUT TODAY:

"DON'T WATCH THE CLOCK. DO WHAT IT DOES — KEEP ON GOING."

DATE : ....

WHAT I LOVED ABOUT TODAY:

"KNOWING IS NOT ENOUGH; WE MUST APPLY.
WILLING IS NOT ENOUGH; WE MUST DO."

WHAT I LOVED ABOUT TODAY:

"BE A WARRIOR, NOT A WORRIER."

DATE : ....

WHAT I LOVED ABOUT TODAY:

"THE ONLY WAY TO DO GREAT WORK IS TO LOVE WHAT YOU DO."

WHAT I LOVED ABOUT TODAY:

"WHEN YOU WANT TO SUCCEED AS MUCH AS YOU WANT TO BREATHE, THAT'S WHEN YOU BECOME SUCCESSFUL."

DATE : ....

WHAT I LOVED ABOUT TODAY:

"PERSISTENCE CAN CHANGE FAILURE INTO
EXTRAORDINARY ACHIEVEMENT."

WHAT I LOVED ABOUT TODAY:

"YESTERDAY YOU SAID TOMORROW."

DATE : ....

WHAT I LOVED ABOUT TODAY:

"SUCCESSFUL PEOPLE NEVER WORRY ABOUT WHAT OTHERS ARE DOING."

WHAT I LOVED ABOUT TODAY:

"I CAN'T CHANGE THE DIRECTION OF THE WIND, BUT I CAN ADJUST MY SAILS TO ALWAYS REACH MY DESTINATION."

DATE : ....

WHAT I LOVED ABOUT TODAY:

"YOU CAN'T HAVE A BETTER TOMORROW IF YOU'RE STILL THINKING ABOUT YESTERDAY."

WHAT I LOVED ABOUT TODAY:

"IF YOU CAN FIND A PATH WITH NO OBSTACLES,
IT PROBABLY DOESN'T LEAD ANYWHERE."

DATE : ....

WHAT I LOVED ABOUT TODAY:

"SOME DAYS YOU JUST HAVE TO CREATE YOUR OWN SUNSHINE."

WHAT I LOVED ABOUT TODAY:

"THE EXPERT IN ANYTHING WAS ONCE A BEGINNER."

DATE : ....

WHAT I LOVED ABOUT TODAY:

"IT DOESN'T MATTER WHO HURT YOU, OR BROKE YOU DOWN. WHAT MATTERS IS WHO MADE YOU SMILE AGAIN."

DATE : ....

WHAT I LOVED ABOUT TODAY:

"LET YOUR SMILE CHANGE THE WORLD, BUT DON'T LET THE WORLD CHANGE YOUR SMILE."

DATE : ....

WHAT I LOVED ABOUT TODAY:

"EVERY ACCOMPLISHMENT STARTS WITH THE DECISION TO TRY."

WHAT I LOVED ABOUT TODAY:

"PRESSURE CAN BURST A PIPE, BUT IT CAN ALSO CREATE DIAMONDS."

DATE : ....

WHAT I LOVED ABOUT TODAY:

"BE A GAME CHANGER: THE WORLD ALREADY HAS ENOUGH FOLLOWERS."

WHAT I LOVED ABOUT TODAY:

"WAKE UP. KICK ASS. REPEAT."

DATE : ....

WHAT I LOVED ABOUT TODAY:

"TAKE A DEEP BREATH. IT'S JUST A BAD
DAY, NOT A BAD LIFE."

WHAT I LOVED ABOUT TODAY:

"PATIENCE IS NOT THE ABILITY TO WAIT, BUT THE ABILITY TO KEEP A GOOD ATTITUDE WHILE WAITING."

DATE : ....

WHAT I LOVED ABOUT TODAY:

"THE ONLY TIME YOU SHOULD EVER LOOK BACK IS TO SEE HOW FAR YOU HAVE COME."

WHAT I LOVED ABOUT TODAY:

"IF THE PLAN DOESN'T WORK, CHANGE THE PLAN —
NOT THE GOAL."

DATE : ....

WHAT I LOVED ABOUT TODAY:

"I DON'T KNOW WHAT THE FUTURE HOLDS, BUT
I DO KNOW WHO HOLDS THE FUTURE."

WHAT I LOVED ABOUT TODAY:

"THERE ARE NO SECRETS TO SUCCESS. IT IS THE RESULT OF PREPARATION, HARD WORK AND LEARNING FROM FAILURE."

DATE : ....

WHAT I LOVED ABOUT TODAY:

"STRIVE NOT TO BE A SUCCESS, BUT TO BE OF VALUE."

WHAT I LOVED ABOUT TODAY:

"DON'T LET THE FEAR OF LOSING BE GREATER THAN THE EXCITEMENT OF WINNING."

DATE : ....

WHAT I LOVED ABOUT TODAY:

"DON'T LET SMALL MINDS CONVINCE YOU THAT YOUR DREAMS ARE TOO BIG."

WHAT I LOVED ABOUT TODAY:

"QUALITY MEANS DOING IT RIGHT WHEN NO ONE IS LOOKING."

DATE : ....

WHAT I LOVED ABOUT TODAY:

> "THINGS DO NOT HAPPEN. THINGS ARE MADE TO HAPPEN."

WHAT I LOVED ABOUT TODAY:

"STRENGTH DOESN'T COME FROM WHAT YOU CAN DO. IT COMES FROM OVERCOMING THE THINGS YOU ONCE THOUGHT YOU COULDN'T DO."

DATE : ....

WHAT I LOVED ABOUT TODAY:

"EVERY CHAMPION WAS ONCE A CONTENDER WHO REFUSED TO GIVE UP."

WHAT I LOVED ABOUT TODAY:

"IF IT DOESN'T CHALLENGE YOU, IT DOESN'T CHANGE YOU."

DATE : ....

WHAT I LOVED ABOUT TODAY:

"THE DREAM IS FREE. THE HUSTLE IS SOLD SEPARATELY."

WHAT I LOVED ABOUT TODAY:

> "TODAY I WILL DO WHAT OTHERS WON'T, SO TOMORROW I CAN DO WHAT OTHERS CAN'T."

DATE : ....

WHAT I LOVED ABOUT TODAY:

"IF OPPORTUNITY DOESN'T KNOCK, BUILD A DOOR."

WHAT I LOVED ABOUT TODAY:

"GO CONFIDENTLY IN THE DIRECTION OF YOUR DREAMS. LIVE THE LIFE YOU HAVE IMAGINED."

DATE : ....

WHAT I LOVED ABOUT TODAY:

"WHAT HURTS MORE — THE PAIN OF HARD WORK, OR THE PAIN OF REGRET?"

WHAT I LOVED ABOUT TODAY:

"KEEP AWAY FROM THOSE WHO TRY TO BELITTLE YOUR AMBITIONS."

DATE : ....

WHAT I LOVED ABOUT TODAY:

"THERE IS ALWAYS ROOM AT THE TOP."

WHAT I LOVED ABOUT TODAY:

"EVERY DAY IS A SECOND CHANCE."

DATE : ....

WHAT I LOVED ABOUT TODAY:

"QUIT TALKING. START DOING."

WHAT I LOVED ABOUT TODAY:

"IN THE END, WE ONLY REGRET THE CHANCES WE DIDN'T TAKE."

DATE : ....

WHAT I LOVED ABOUT TODAY:

"NO MATTER HOW YOU FEEL, GET UP, DRESS UP,
SHOW UP AND NEVER GIVE UP."

DATE : ....

WHAT I LOVED ABOUT TODAY:

"EVERY JOB IS A SELF-PORTRAIT OF THE PERSON WHO DOES IT. AUTOGRAPH YOUR WORK WITH EXCELLENCE."

DATE : ....

WHAT I LOVED ABOUT TODAY:

"ARRIVING AT ONE GOAL IS THE STARTING POINT FOR ANOTHER."

WHAT I LOVED ABOUT TODAY:

"A SMOOTH SEA NEVER MADE A SKILLFUL SAILER."

DATE : ....

WHAT I LOVED ABOUT TODAY:

```
"DO YOUR BEST AND FORGET THE REST."
```

WHAT I LOVED ABOUT TODAY:

"IT ALWAYS SEEMS IMPOSSIBLE UNTIL IT'S DONE."

DATE : ....

WHAT I LOVED ABOUT TODAY:

"THINK POSITIVE, AND POSITIVE THINGS WILL HAPPEN."

WHAT I LOVED ABOUT TODAY:

"SLOW PROGRESS IS BETTER THAN NO PROGRESS."

DATE : ....

WHAT I LOVED ABOUT TODAY:

"BE YOURSELF AND QUIT TRYING TO BE EVERYONE ELSE."

WHAT I LOVED ABOUT TODAY:

"COURAGE IS TAKING THOSE FIRST STEPS TO YOUR DREAM. EVEN IF YOU CAN'T SEE THE PATH AHEAD."

DATE : ....

WHAT I LOVED ABOUT TODAY:

"TO LIVE IS THE RAREST THING ON EARTH. MOST PEOPLE JUST EXIST."

WHAT I LOVED ABOUT TODAY:

> "DON'T QUIT. SUFFER NOW AND LIVE THE REST OF YOUR LIFE AS A CHAMPION."

DATE : ....

WHAT I LOVED ABOUT TODAY:

"WHATEVER THE MIND CAN CONCEIVE AND
BELIEVE, IT CAN ACHIEVE."

WHAT I LOVED ABOUT TODAY:

"THE FUTURE BELONGS TO THOSE WHO BELIEVE
IN THE BEAUTY OF THEIR DREAMS."

DATE : ....

WHAT I LOVED ABOUT TODAY:

"IT'S NOT ABOUT BEING THE BEST. IT'S ABOUT
BEING BETTER THAN YOU WERE YESTERDAY."

WHAT I LOVED ABOUT TODAY:

"DO IT BECAUSE THEY SAID YOU COULDN'T."

DATE : ....

WHAT I LOVED ABOUT TODAY:

"EITHER YOU RUN THE DAY OR THE DAY RUNS YOU."

WHAT I LOVED ABOUT TODAY:

"YOU ARE ONLY CONFINED BY THE WALLS YOU BUILD YOURSELF."

DATE : ....

WHAT I LOVED ABOUT TODAY:

"I'M NOT HERE TO BE AVERAGE. I'M HERE TO BE AWESOME."

WHAT I LOVED ABOUT TODAY:

.

"YOUR LIFE IS YOUR MESSAGE TO THE WORLD. MAKE SURE IT'S INSPIRING."

DATE : ....

WHAT I LOVED ABOUT TODAY:

"THERE IS NO "I" IN TEAM, BUT THERE IS IN WIN."

WHAT I LOVED ABOUT TODAY:

```
"LIFE BEGINS AT THE END OF YOUR COMFORT ZONE."
```

DATE : ....

WHAT I LOVED ABOUT TODAY:

"MAKE TODAY RIDICULOUSLY AMAZING."

WHAT I LOVED ABOUT TODAY:

"WHENEVER ANYONE HAS OFFENDED ME. I TRY TO RAISE MY SOUL SO HIGH THAT THE OFFENSE CAN NOT REACH IT."

DATE : ....

WHAT I LOVED ABOUT TODAY:

"WHAT WOULD YOU ATTEMPT TO DO IF
YOU KNEW YOU COULD NOT FAIL?"

WHAT I LOVED ABOUT TODAY:

"THE DISTANCE BETWEEN YOUR DREAM AND REALITY IS CALLED ACTION."

DATE : ....

WHAT I LOVED ABOUT TODAY:

"BE SO BUSY IMPROVING YOURSELF THAT YOU HAVE NO TIME TO CRITICIZE OTHERS."

WHAT I LOVED ABOUT TODAY:

"LIFE IS TOO SHORT TO WAIT."

DATE : ....

WHAT I LOVED ABOUT TODAY:

"EDUCATION IS THE MOST POWERFUL WEAPON
WE CAN USE TO CHANGE THE WORLD."

WHAT I LOVED ABOUT TODAY:

"BE THE TYPE OF PERSON YOU WANT TO MEET."

DATE : ....

WHAT I LOVED ABOUT TODAY:

"A MOTIVATED MAN IS MOTIVATED BY THE DESIRE TO ACHIEVE, NOT BY THE DESIRE TO BEAT OTHERS."

DATE : ....

WHAT I LOVED ABOUT TODAY:

> "MOST POWERFUL IS HE WHO HAS HIMSELF
> IN HIS OWN POWER."

DATE : ....

WHAT I LOVED ABOUT TODAY:

"THERE IS NO ONE GIANT STEP. IT'S LOTS OF LITTLE STEPS."

WHAT I LOVED ABOUT TODAY:

"ENJOY THE LITTLE THINGS IN LIFE... FOR ONE DAY YOU'LL LOOK BACK AND REALIZE THEY WERE THE BIG THINGS."

DATE : ....

WHAT I LOVED ABOUT TODAY:

"YOU CAN'T PUT A LIMIT ON ANYTHING."

WHAT I LOVED ABOUT TODAY:

"CHOP YOUR OWN WOOD AND IT WILL WARM YOU TWICE."

DATE : ....

WHAT I LOVED ABOUT TODAY:

"YOU'LL BE SURPRISED TO KNOW HOW FAR YOU CAN GO FROM THE POINT WHERE YOU THOUGHT IT WAS THE END."

WHAT I LOVED ABOUT TODAY:

"SOME PEOPLE CREATE THEIR OWN STORMS, THEN GET UPSET WHEN IT RAINS."

DATE : ....

WHAT I LOVED ABOUT TODAY:

"ALWAYS END THE DAY WITH A POSITIVE THOUGHT."

WHAT I LOVED ABOUT TODAY:

"WAKE UP, SMILE AND TELL YOURSELF TODAY IS MY DAY."

DATE : ....

WHAT I LOVED ABOUT TODAY:

"THE BEST IS YET TO COME."

WHAT I LOVED ABOUT TODAY:

"ONLY IN THE DARKNESS CAN YOU SEE THE STARS."

DATE : ....

WHAT I LOVED ABOUT TODAY:

"YOUR MIND IS A POWERFUL THING. WHEN YOU FILL IT WITH POSITIVE THOUGHTS, YOUR LIFE WILL START TO CHANGE."

WHAT I LOVED ABOUT TODAY:

"SURROUND YOURSELF BY PEOPLE WHO ARE GOING TO LIFT YOU HIGHER."

DATE : ....

WHAT I LOVED ABOUT TODAY:

"DO THE DIFFICULT THINGS WHEN THEY ARE EASY AND DO THE GREAT THINGS WHILE THEY ARE SMALL."

WHAT I LOVED ABOUT TODAY:

"IN ORDER TO CARRY A POSITIVE ACTION, WE MUST DEVELOP HERE A POSITIVE VISION."

DATE : ....

WHAT I LOVED ABOUT TODAY:

"HAPPINESS CAN BE FOUND, EVEN IN THE DARKEST OF TIMES, IF ONE ONLY REMEMBERS TO TURN ON THE LIGHT."

WHAT I LOVED ABOUT TODAY:

"CONFIDENCE IS NOT 'THEY WILL LIKE ME', IT'S 'I'LL BE FINE IF THEY DON'T'."

DATE : ....

WHAT I LOVED ABOUT TODAY:

"IT MAY BE STORMY NOW, BUT IT NEVER RAINS FOREVER."

WHAT I LOVED ABOUT TODAY:

"NEGATIVE PEOPLE NEED DRAMA LIKE OXYGEN. STAY POSITIVE, IT WILL TAKE THEIR BREATH AWAY."

DATE : ....

WHAT I LOVED ABOUT TODAY:

"YOU HAVE 86,400 SECONDS TODAY. HOW WILL YOU USE THEM?"

WHAT I LOVED ABOUT TODAY:

"THOSE WHO DON'T BELIEVE IN MAGIC WILL NEVER FIND IT."

DATE : ....

WHAT I LOVED ABOUT TODAY:

"BE THE CHANGE YOU WANT TO SEE IN THE WORLD."

WHAT I LOVED ABOUT TODAY:

"YOU CAN'T APPRECIATE THE GOOD DAYS WITHOUT THE BAD ONES."

DATE : ....

WHAT I LOVED ABOUT TODAY:

"STOP LOOKING FOR HAPPINESS IN THE SAME PLACE YOU LOST IT."

WHAT I LOVED ABOUT TODAY:

"YOU ARE STRONGER THAN YOU SEEM, BRAVER THAN YOU BELIEVE, AND SMARTER THAN YOU THINK YOU ARE."

DATE : ....

WHAT I LOVED ABOUT TODAY:

"ONE SMALL POSITIVE THOUGHT IN THE
MORNING CAN CHANGE YOUR ENTIRE DAY."

WHAT I LOVED ABOUT TODAY:

"WHEN EVERYTHING SEEMS LIKE AN UPHILL STRUGGLE,
JUST THINK OF THE VIEW FROM THE TOP."

DATE : ....

WHAT I LOVED ABOUT TODAY:

"TALKING ABOUT OUR PROBLEMS IS OUR GREATEST ADDICTION. BREAK THE HABIT. TALK ABOUT YOUR JOYS."

WHAT I LOVED ABOUT TODAY:

"ONE KIND WORD CAN CHANGE SOMEONE'S ENTIRE DAY."

DATE : ....

WHAT I LOVED ABOUT TODAY:

"WE MAY ENCOUNTER MANY DEFEATS, BUT
WE MUST NOT BE DEFEATED."

DATE : ....

WHAT I LOVED ABOUT TODAY:

"CHALLENGES ARE WHAT MAKE LIFE INTERESTING, AND OVERCOMING THEM IS WHAT MAKES LIFE MEANINGFUL"

DATE : ....

WHAT I LOVED ABOUT TODAY:

"YOUR MISTAKES DO NOT DEFINE YOU."

DATE : ....

WHAT I LOVED ABOUT TODAY:

> "BE IN LOVE WITH YOUR LIFE."

DATE : ....

WHAT I LOVED ABOUT TODAY:

"YOU WERE GIVEN THIS LIFE BECAUSE YOU WERE STRONG ENOUGH TO LIVE IT."

WHAT I LOVED ABOUT TODAY:

"SUCCESS IS HOW HIGH YOU BOUNCE WHEN YOU HIT THE BOTTOM."

DATE : ....

WHAT I LOVED ABOUT TODAY:

"TRY AND FAIL. DON'T FAIL TO TRY."

WHAT I LOVED ABOUT TODAY:

"THE DARKEST HOUR HAS ONLY 60 MINUTES."

DATE : ....

WHAT I LOVED ABOUT TODAY:

"BE PROUD OF WHO YOU ARE AND NOT ASHAMED OF HOW SOMEONE ELSE SEES YOU."

DATE : ....

WHAT I LOVED ABOUT TODAY:

"A CERTAIN DARKNESS IS NEEDED TO SEE THE STARS."

DATE : ....

WHAT I LOVED ABOUT TODAY:

"TURN YOUR CAN'TS INTO CANS AND YOUR DREAMS INTO PLANS."

WHAT I LOVED ABOUT TODAY:

"YOU CAN'T LIVE A POSITIVE LIFE WITH A NEGATIVE MIND."

DATE : ....

WHAT I LOVED ABOUT TODAY:

"LIFE IS YOUR MIRROR. WHAT YOU SEE AS YOUR OUTSIDE ALWAYS COMES FROM THE INSIDE."

WHAT I LOVED ABOUT TODAY:

"THERE IS NO PASSION TO BE FOUND IN SETTLING FOR A
LIFE THAT IS LESS THAN YOU ARE CAPABLE OF LIVING."

DATE : ....

WHAT I LOVED ABOUT TODAY:

"BE SO GOOD THEY CAN'T IGNORE YOU."

WHAT I LOVED ABOUT TODAY:

> "TAKE TIME TODAY TO APPRECIATE SOMEONE WHO DOES SOMETHING YOU TAKE FOR GRANTED."

DATE : ....

WHAT I LOVED ABOUT TODAY:

"THE HAPPIEST PEOPLE DON'T HAVE THE BEST OF EVERYTHING,
THEY JUST MAKE THE MOST OF EVERYTHING."

WHAT I LOVED ABOUT TODAY:

"LIFE'S A JOURNEY, NOT A RACE."

DATE : ....

WHAT I LOVED ABOUT TODAY:

"IF EVERYBODY LIKES WHAT YOU'RE DOING,
YOU'RE DOING IT WRONG."

WHAT I LOVED ABOUT TODAY:

"DON'T BE AFRAID OF CHANGE, IT IS LEADING YOU TO A NEW BEGINNING."

DATE : ....

WHAT I LOVED ABOUT TODAY:

"SOME PEOPLE DREAM OF SUCCESS, WHILE OTHERS
WAKE UP AND WORK HARD FOR IT."

WHAT I LOVED ABOUT TODAY:

"YOU'LL NEVER CHANGE YOUR LIFE UNTIL YOU CHANGE SOMETHING YOU DO DAILY. THE SECRET OF YOUR SUCCESS IS FOUND IN YOUR DAILY ROUTINE."

DATE : ....

WHAT I LOVED ABOUT TODAY:

"WORRY LESS, GIGGLE MORE."

WHAT I LOVED ABOUT TODAY:

"DON'T CHASE PEOPLE: BE YOU. DO YOUR OWN THING AND WORK HARD. THE RIGHT PEOPLE WHO BELONG IN YOUR LIFE WILL COME TO YOU. AND STAY."

DATE : ....

WHAT I LOVED ABOUT TODAY:

"THERE IS ONLY ONE CORNER OF THE UNIVERSE YOU CAN
BE CERTAIN OF IMPROVING, AND THAT'S YOUR SELF."

WHAT I LOVED ABOUT TODAY:

"THE GREATEST PLEASURE IN LIFE IS DOING WHAT OTHERS SAY YOU CANNOT DO."

DATE : ....

WHAT I LOVED ABOUT TODAY:

"THE PAST SHOULD BE THE PAST. IT CAN DESTROY THE FUTURE. LIVE LIFE FOR WHAT TOMORROW HAS TO OFFER, NOT FOR WHAT YESTERDAY HAS TAKEN AWAY."

WHAT I LOVED ABOUT TODAY:

"DON'T WORRY ABOUT THOSE WHO TALK BEHIND YOUR BACK. THEY'RE BEHIND YOU FOR A REASON."

DATE : ....

WHAT I LOVED ABOUT TODAY:

"IT'S OK TO BE A GLOWSTICK. SOMETIMES WE HAVE TO BREAK BEFORE WE SHINE."

WHAT I LOVED ABOUT TODAY:

"COURAGE IS WHAT IT TAKES TO STAND UP AND SPEAK. COURAGE IS ALSO WHAT IT TAKES TO SIT DOWN AND LISTEN."

DATE : ....

WHAT I LOVED ABOUT TODAY:

"IF YOU DON'T GO AFTER WHAT YOU WANT, YOU WILL NEVER HAVE IT. IF YOU DON'T ASK, THE ANSWER WILL ALWAYS BE NO. IF YOU DON'T STEP FORWARD, YOU'RE ALWAYS IN THE SAME PLACE."

WHAT I LOVED ABOUT TODAY:

"THE STRUGGLE YOU'RE IN TODAY IS DEVELOPING THE STRENGTH YOU NEED FOR TOMORROW."

DATE : ....

WHAT I LOVED ABOUT TODAY:

"EVERY DAY THERE IS SAD NEWS AND BAD NEWS,
BUT EACH DAY ITSELF IS GLAD NEWS."

DATE : ....

WHAT I LOVED ABOUT TODAY:

"LIFE CAN BE UNFAIR SOMETIMES, BUT THAT'S NO REASON TO GIVE UP ON IT."

DATE : ....

WHAT I LOVED ABOUT TODAY:

"ANY INTELLIGENT FOOL CAN MAKE THINGS BIGGER AND MORE COMPLEX... IT TAKES A TOUCH OF GENIUS — AND A LOT OF COURAGE — TO MOVE IN THE OPPOSITE DIRECTION."

WHAT I LOVED ABOUT TODAY:

"TRUST YOURSELF. YOU KNOW MORE THAN YOU THINK YOU DO."

DATE : ....

WHAT I LOVED ABOUT TODAY:

"MY DESIRE TO SUCCEED IS MORE POWERFUL
THAN DISAPPOINTMENT."

WHAT I LOVED ABOUT TODAY:

"DON'T LET INSECURITY RUIN THE BEAUTY YOU WERE BORN WITH."

DATE : ....

WHAT I LOVED ABOUT TODAY:

"I'M GOING TO MAKE THE REST OF MY LIFE, THE
BEST OF MY LIFE."

WHAT I LOVED ABOUT TODAY:

"DON'T LOOK BACK — YOU'RE NOT GOING THAT WAY."

DATE : ....

WHAT I LOVED ABOUT TODAY:

"THERE WILL BE OBSTACLES, THERE WILL BE DOUBTERS, THERE WILL BE MISTAKES. BUT WITH HARD WORK, THERE ARE NO LIMITS."

WHAT I LOVED ABOUT TODAY:

"ALL ROADS THAT LEAD TO SUCCESS HAVE TO PASS THROUGH HARDWORK BOULEVARD FIRST."

DATE : ....

WHAT I LOVED ABOUT TODAY:

"DON'T GIVE UP WHAT YOU WANT MOST FOR WHAT YOU WANT NOW."

WHAT I LOVED ABOUT TODAY:

"IF YOU ARE WAITING FOR THE RIGHT TIME, IT'S NOW."

DATE : ....

WHAT I LOVED ABOUT TODAY:

"YOU ONLY LIVE ONCE? FALSE. YOU LIVE EVERYDAY.
YOU ONLY DIE ONCE."

WHAT I LOVED ABOUT TODAY:

"UNLESS YOU PUKE, FAINT OR DIE — KEEP ON GOING."

DATE : ....

WHAT I LOVED ABOUT TODAY:

```
"YOU DON'T NEED A REASON TO HELP PEOPLE."
```

WHAT I LOVED ABOUT TODAY:

"WHAT'S STOPPING YOU? THAT'S RIGHT — NOTHING."

DATE : ....

WHAT I LOVED ABOUT TODAY:

"VICTORY BELONGS TO THE MOST PERSEVERING."

WHAT I LOVED ABOUT TODAY:

"YOU'RE A DIAMOND, DEAR. THEY CAN'T BREAK YOU."

DATE : ....

WHAT I LOVED ABOUT TODAY:

"WORRYING DOES NOT EMPTY TOMORROW OF ITS TROUBLES.
IT EMPTIES TODAY OF ITS STRENGTH."

WHAT I LOVED ABOUT TODAY:

"DON'T LET ANYONE DULL YOUR SPARKLE."

DATE : ....

WHAT I LOVED ABOUT TODAY:

"FORGET ALL THE REASONS WHY IT WON'T WORK
AND BELIEVE THE ONE REASON WHY IT WILL."

DATE : ....

WHAT I LOVED ABOUT TODAY:

"NOBODY MAKES YOU ANGRY, YOU DECIDE TO USE
ANGER AS A RESPONSE."

DATE : ....

WHAT I LOVED ABOUT TODAY:

"INHALE THE GOOD SHIT, EXHALE THE BULLSHIT."

WHAT I LOVED ABOUT TODAY:

"THINK LIKE A PROTON AND STAY POSITIVE."

DATE : ....

WHAT I LOVED ABOUT TODAY:

"KEEP YOUR EYES ON THE STARS AND YOUR FEET ON THE GROUND."

WHAT I LOVED ABOUT TODAY:

"STRESSED SPELLED BACKWARDS IS DESSERT."

DATE : ....

WHAT I LOVED ABOUT TODAY:

"YOU DON'T ALWAYS NEED A PLAN. SOMETIMES YOU JUST NEED TO BREATHE, TRUST, LET GO, AND SEE WHAT HAPPENS."

DATE : ....

WHAT I LOVED ABOUT TODAY:

"POSITIVE MIND. POSITIVE VIBES. POSITIVE LIFE."

DATE : ....

WHAT I LOVED ABOUT TODAY:

"BELIEVE THAT LIFE IS WORTH LIVING AND YOUR BELIEF WILL HELP CREATE THE FACT."

DATE : ....

WHAT I LOVED ABOUT TODAY:

"FEAR KILLS MORE DREAMS THAN FAILURE EVER WILL."

225

DATE : ....

WHAT I LOVED ABOUT TODAY:

"THE CREATIVE ADULT IS THE CHILD WHO SURVIVED."

WHAT I LOVED ABOUT TODAY:

"YOU CAN'T START THE NEW CHAPTER OF YOUR LIFE
IF YOU KEEP RE-READING THE LAST ONE."

DATE : ....

WHAT I LOVED ABOUT TODAY:

"WHEN ONE DOOR OF HAPPINESS CLOSES, ANOTHER OPENS; BUT OFTEN WE LOOK SO LONG AT THE CLOSED DOORS THAT WE DO NOT SEE THE ONE WHICH HAS BEEN OPENED FOR US."

WHAT I LOVED ABOUT TODAY:

"LIFE IS ALL ABOUT FINDING PEOPLE WHO ARE YOUR KIND OF CRAZY."

DATE : ....

WHAT I LOVED ABOUT TODAY:

WHAT I LOVED ABOUT TODAY:

"THINK A LITTLE LESS. LIVE A LITTLE MORE."

DATE : ....

WHAT I LOVED ABOUT TODAY:

"COUNT YOUR BLESSINGS, NOT YOUR PROBLEMS."

WHAT I LOVED ABOUT TODAY:

"EVERY THOUGHT WE THINK IS CREATING OUR FUTURE."

DATE : ....

WHAT I LOVED ABOUT TODAY:

"RIGHT NOW, SOMEONE OUT THERE IS WONDERING WHAT IT'S LIKE TO KNOW SOMEONE LIKE ME."

WHAT I LOVED ABOUT TODAY:

"IF SOMEONE IS STRONG ENOUGH TO BRING YOU DOWN,
SHOW THEM YOU'RE STRONG ENOUGH TO GET BACK UP."

DATE : ....

WHAT I LOVED ABOUT TODAY:

"LIFE IS LIKE PHOTOGRAPHY. WE DEVELOP FROM
THE NEGATIVES."

WHAT I LOVED ABOUT TODAY:

"LIFE ISN'T ABOUT WAITING FOR THE STORM TO PASS...
IT'S LEARNING TO DANCE IN THE RAIN."

DATE : ....

WHAT I LOVED ABOUT TODAY:

WHAT I LOVED ABOUT TODAY:

"A WISH CHANGES NOTHING. A DECISION CHANGES EVERYTHING."

DATE : ....

WHAT I LOVED ABOUT TODAY:

"EVEN TOO MUCH SUNSHINE CAN BE DEVASTATING, WHILE ONLY WITH RAIN CAN GROWTH OCCUR. ACCEPT BOTH AS PART OF THE GROWING PROCESS IN THE GARDEN OF LIFE."

WHAT I LOVED ABOUT TODAY:

"EVERYTHING WILL BE OK IN THE END. IF IT'S NOT OK, IT'S NOT THE END."

DATE : ....

WHAT I LOVED ABOUT TODAY:

"WHEN SOMEONE WALKS OUT OF YOUR LIFE, LET THEM. THEY'RE JUST MAKING ROOM FOR SOMEONE BETTER TO WALK IN."

WHAT I LOVED ABOUT TODAY:

"THERE ARE TWO WAYS OF SPREADING LIGHT — TO BE
THE CANDLE, OR THE MIRROR THAT REFLECTS THAT."

DATE : ....

WHAT I LOVED ABOUT TODAY:

"SHIPS IN HARBOURS ARE SAFE, BUT THAT'S NOT WHAT SHIPS WERE BUILT FOR."

WHAT I LOVED ABOUT TODAY:

"THE PAST IS WHERE YOU LEARNED THE LESSON, THE FUTURE IS WHERE YOU APPLY THE LESSON. DON'T GIVE UP IN THE MIDDLE."

DATE : ....

WHAT I LOVED ABOUT TODAY:

"WHEN YOU REACH THE END OF YOUR ROPE,
TIE A KNOT IN IT AND HANG ON."

WHAT I LOVED ABOUT TODAY:

"GOOD, BETTER, BEST. NEVER LET IT REST. 'TIL GOOD IS BETTER AND YOUR BETTER IS BEST."

DATE : ....

WHAT I LOVED ABOUT TODAY:

"DON'T FOLLOW THE CROWD, LET THE CROWD FOLLOW YOU."

WHAT I LOVED ABOUT TODAY:

"POSITIVE THINKING CREATES A DOORWAY THROUGH WHICH ANGELS LOVE TO WALK."

DATE : ....

WHAT I LOVED ABOUT TODAY:

"RESPECT YOURSELF ENOUGH TO WALK AWAY FROM
ANYTHING THAT NO LONGER SERVES YOU, GROWS
YOU OR MAKES YOU HAPPY."

DATE : ....

WHAT I LOVED ABOUT TODAY:

> "DON'T LOOK BACK — YOU MIGHT FALL OVER WHAT IS RIGHT IN FRONT OF YOU."

DATE : ....

WHAT I LOVED ABOUT TODAY:

"LIVE WITHOUT PRETENDING, LOVE WITHOUT DEPENDING, LISTEN WITHOUT DEFENDING AND SPEAK WITHOUT OFFENDING."

WHAT I LOVED ABOUT TODAY:

"NEVER WAIT FOR THE PERFECT MOMENT. USE THE MOMENT AND MAKE IT PERFECT."

DATE : ....

WHAT I LOVED ABOUT TODAY:

"BEFORE YOU POINT THE FINGER, MAKE SURE YOUR HANDS ARE CLEAN."

WHAT I LOVED ABOUT TODAY:

"BETTER THAN A THOUSAND HOLLOW WORDS,
IS ONE WORD THAT BRINGS PEACE."

DATE : ....

WHAT I LOVED ABOUT TODAY:

"IF YOU CAN'T STAND FOR SOMETHING, YOU WILL FALL FOR ANYTHING."

WHAT I LOVED ABOUT TODAY:

"A SMILE IS THE CHEAPEST WAY TO IMPROVE YOUR LOOKS, EVEN IF YOUR TEETH ARE CROOKED."

DATE : ....

WHAT I LOVED ABOUT TODAY:

"I'VE LEARNED SO MUCH FROM MY MISTAKES... THAT I'M THINKING OF MAKING SOME MORE."

WHAT I LOVED ABOUT TODAY:

"DREAM, BUT ALWAYS WITH YOUR EYES WIDE OPEN."

DATE : ....

WHAT I LOVED ABOUT TODAY:

> "YOU KNOW YOU HAVE EVERYTHING WHEN YOU HAVE NOTHING TO LOSE."

DATE : ....

WHAT I LOVED ABOUT TODAY:

"YESTERDAY'S THE PAST, TOMORROW'S THE FUTURE,
BUT TODAY IS THE GIFT. THAT'S WHY THEY CALL IT
THE PRESENT."

DATE : ....

WHAT I LOVED ABOUT TODAY:

"SACRIFICE IS WILLING TO GIVE UP SOMETHING GOOD FOR SOMETHING BETTER."

DATE : ....

WHAT I LOVED ABOUT TODAY:

"PAIN IS TEMPORARY, QUITTING IS FOREVER."

DATE : ....

WHAT I LOVED ABOUT TODAY:

"BE POSITIVE, PATIENT AND PERSISTENT."

WHAT I LOVED ABOUT TODAY:

"WITHOUT LOVE, WE ARE BIRDS WITH BROKEN WINGS."

DATE : ....

WHAT I LOVED ABOUT TODAY:

"WHAT GOES AROUND, COMES AROUND. KEEP YOUR CIRCLE POSITIVE."

DATE : ....

WHAT I LOVED ABOUT TODAY:

"HAPPINESS IS PUTTING MORE EFFORT INTO YOUR INTENTIONS RATHER THAN YOUR EXPECTATIONS."

DATE : ....

WHAT I LOVED ABOUT TODAY:

"ACCEPT THE CHALLENGES SO THAT YOU CAN FEEL THE EXHILARATION OF VICTORY."

DATE : ....

WHAT I LOVED ABOUT TODAY:

"TEACH THE TRIPLE TRUTH TO ALL: A GENEROUS HEART,
KIND SPEECH, AND A LIFE OF SERVICE AND COMPASSION
ARE THE THINGS WHICH RENEW HUMANITY."

DATE : ....

WHAT I LOVED ABOUT TODAY:

"LIVE AS IF YOU WERE GOING TO DIE TOMORROW.
LEARN AS IF YOU WERE TO LIVE FOREVER."

WHAT I LOVED ABOUT TODAY:

"A STRONG POSITIVE MENTAL ATTITUDE WILL CREATE MORE MIRACLES THAN ANY WONDER DRUG."

DATE : ....

WHAT I LOVED ABOUT TODAY:

"ABILITY IS WHAT YOU ARE CAPABLE OF DOING. MOTIVATION DETERMINES WHAT YOU DO. ATTITUDE DETERMINES HOW WELL YOU DO IT."

DATE : ....

WHAT I LOVED ABOUT TODAY:

"EFFORTS AND COURAGE ARE NOT ENOUGH
WITHOUT PURPOSE AND DIRECTION."

DATE : ....

WHAT I LOVED ABOUT TODAY:

"IF YOUR ACTIONS INSPIRE OTHERS TO DREAM MORE, LEARN MORE, DO MORE AND BECOME MORE, YOU ARE A LEADER."

WHAT I LOVED ABOUT TODAY:

"TOO MANY PEOPLE OVERVALUE WHAT THEY ARE
NOT AND UNDERVALUE WHAT THEY ARE."

DATE : ....

WHAT I LOVED ABOUT TODAY:

"A MIRACLE IS A SHIFT IN PERCEPTION FROM FEAR TO LOVE."

WHAT I LOVED ABOUT TODAY:

"YOU HAVE THE POWER TO FEEL ANY WAY YOU CHOOSE. SO CHOOSE TO FEEL WONDERFUL."

DATE : ....

WHAT I LOVED ABOUT TODAY:

"IMPERFECTION IS BEAUTY. MADNESS IS GENIUS. AND IT'S BETTER TO BE ABSOLUTELY RIDICULOUS THAN ABSOLUTELY BORING."

DATE : ....

WHAT I LOVED ABOUT TODAY:

> "WITHOUT PEACE, ALL OTHER DREAMS VANISH
> AND ARE REDUCED TO ASHES."

DATE : ....

WHAT I LOVED ABOUT TODAY:

"HAPPINESS IS THE SELLING OF THE SOUL INTO ITS MOST APPROPRIATE SPOT."

WHAT I LOVED ABOUT TODAY:

"THE DIFFERENCE BETWEEN A SUCCESSFUL PERSON AND OTHERS IS NOT A LACK OF STRENGTH, NOT A LACK OF KNOWLEDGE, BUT RATHER A LACK OF WILL."

DATE : ....

WHAT I LOVED ABOUT TODAY:

"NOT ALL WHO WANDER ARE LOST."

WHAT I LOVED ABOUT TODAY:

"THE JOURNEY IS THE REWARD."

DATE : ....

WHAT I LOVED ABOUT TODAY:

"LEARN FROM YESTERDAY, LIVE FOR TODAY, HOPE FOR TOMORROW. THE IMPORTANT   THING IS NOT TO STOP QUESTIONING."

WHAT I LOVED ABOUT TODAY:

"PEOPLE MAY DOUBT WHAT YOU SAY, BUT THEY'LL BELIEVE WHAT YOU DO."

DATE : ....

WHAT I LOVED ABOUT TODAY:

"FOCUS. DETERMINATION. DOMINATION."

WHAT I LOVED ABOUT TODAY:

"SHOWING YOUR EMOTIONS IS A SIGN OF STRENGTH."

DATE : ....

WHAT I LOVED ABOUT TODAY:

"LET US SACRIFICE TODAY SO THAT OUR CHILDREN
CAN HAVE A BETTER TOMORROW."

WHAT I LOVED ABOUT TODAY:

"HEALTH IS THE GREATEST GIFT, CONTENTMENT THE GREATEST WEALTH, FAITHFULNESS THE BEST RELATIONSHIP."

DATE : ....

WHAT I LOVED ABOUT TODAY:

"I CAN IS A THOUSAND TIMES MORE IMPORTANT THAN IQ."

WHAT I LOVED ABOUT TODAY:

"SUCCESS CONSISTS OF DOING THE COMMON THINGS OF LIFE UNCOMMONLY WELL."

DATE : ....

WHAT I LOVED ABOUT TODAY:

"OPEN YOUR EYES, LOOK WITHIN. ARE YOU SATISFIED WITH THE LIFE YOU'RE LIVING?"

WHAT I LOVED ABOUT TODAY:

"POSITIVE THINKING EVOKES MORE ENERGY, MORE INITIATIVE, MORE HAPPINESS."

DATE : ....

WHAT I LOVED ABOUT TODAY:

"DO NOT WAIT FOR LEADERS, DO IT ALONE —
PERSON TO PERSON."

WHAT I LOVED ABOUT TODAY:

"A LEADER IS A DEALER IN HOPE."

DATE : ....

WHAT I LOVED ABOUT TODAY:

"DREAMS DON'T WORK UNLESS YOU DO."

WHAT I LOVED ABOUT TODAY:

"BEFORE ASKING SOMEONE WHY THEY HATE YOU,
ASK YOURSELF WHY YOU EVEN REALLY CARE."

DATE : ....

WHAT I LOVED ABOUT TODAY:

"WE JUDGE OURSELVES BY WHAT WE FEEL
CAPABLE OF DOING, WHILE OTHERS JUDGE US
BY WHAT WE HAVE ALREADY DONE."

WHAT I LOVED ABOUT TODAY:

"NEVER APOLOGIZE FOR SHOWING FEELINGS. BY DOING SO, YOU APOLOGIZE FOR THE TRUTH."

DATE : ....

WHAT I LOVED ABOUT TODAY:

"LIFE IS INFINITELY STRANGER THAN ANYTHING THE MIND COULD INVENT."

WHAT I LOVED ABOUT TODAY:

"SOME RELATIONSHIPS ARE LIKE GLASS. IT IS BETTER TO LEAVE IT BROKEN THAN TO HURT YOURSELF MORE BY TRYING TO PUT IT BACK TOGETHER."

DATE : ....

WHAT I LOVED ABOUT TODAY:

> "KEEP SMILING AND ONE DAY LIFE WILL GET TIRED OF UPSETTING YOU."

WHAT I LOVED ABOUT TODAY:

"IF YOU EXPECT THE WORLD TO BE FAIR WITH YOU BECAUSE YOU ARE FAIR, YOU'RE FOOLING YOURSELF. THAT'S LIKE EXPECTING THE LION NOT TO EAT YOU BECAUSE YOU DIDN'T EAT HIM."

DATE : ....

WHAT I LOVED ABOUT TODAY:

"IT IS PERFECTLY OK TO ADMIT YOU'RE NOT OK."

WHAT I LOVED ABOUT TODAY:

"THE STRONGEST PEOPLE ARE NOT THOSE WHO SHOW STRENGTH IN FRONT OF US, BUT THOSE WHO WIN BATTLES WE KNOW NOTHING ABOUT."

DATE : ....

WHAT I LOVED ABOUT TODAY:

"LIFE IS A STRANGE GAME. THE ONLY WINNING MOVE IS NOT TO PLAY."

WHAT I LOVED ABOUT TODAY:

"THE NAKED TRUTH IS ALWAYS BETTER THAN
THE BEST-DRESSED LIE."

DATE : ....

WHAT I LOVED ABOUT TODAY:

"THE ONLY WORDS YOU'LL REGRET MORE THAN THE ONES LEFT UNSAID ARE THE ONES YOU USED TO INTENTIONALLY HURT SOMEONE."

WHAT I LOVED ABOUT TODAY:

"THINGS WILL GET WORSE BEFORE THEY GET BETTER. BUT WHEN THEY DO, REMEMBER WHO PUT YOU DOWN, AND WHO HELPED YOU UP."

DATE : ....

WHAT I LOVED ABOUT TODAY:

WHAT I LOVED ABOUT TODAY:

"A SECOND CHANCE DOESN'T MEAN ANYTHING IF YOU HAVEN'T LEARNED FROM YOUR FIRST MISTAKE."

DATE : ....

WHAT I LOVED ABOUT TODAY:

"WEAK PEOPLE REVENGE. STRONG PEOPLE FORGIVE.
INTELLIGENT PEOPLE IGNORE."

DATE : ....

WHAT I LOVED ABOUT TODAY:

```
"PEOPLE WAIT ALL WEEK FOR FRIDAY, ALL YEAR
FOR SUMMER, ALL LIFE FOR HAPPINESS."
```

DATE : ....

WHAT I LOVED ABOUT TODAY:

"RESPECT PEOPLE WHO FIND TIME FOR YOU IN THEIR BUSY SCHEDULE. BUT LOVE PEOPLE WHO NEVER LOOK AT THEIR SCHEDULE WHEN YOU NEED THEM."

WHAT I LOVED ABOUT TODAY:

"YOUR PAST IS JUST A STORY. AND ONCE YOU REALIZE THIS, IT HAS NO POWER OVER YOU."

DATE : ....

WHAT I LOVED ABOUT TODAY:

"FORGIVE THEM AND FORGET THEM. HOLDING ONTO
ANGER AND BITTERNESS CONSUMES YOU NOT THEM."

WHAT I LOVED ABOUT TODAY:

"GREATNESS IS BEST MEASURED BY HOW WELL AN INDIVIDUAL RESPONDS TO THE HAPPENINGS IN LIFE THAT APPEAR TO BE TOTALLY UNFAIR, UNREASONABLE, AND UNDESERVED."

DATE : ....

WHAT I LOVED ABOUT TODAY:

"LIFE DOESN'T ALWAYS GIVE YOU SECOND CHANCES, SO TAKE THE FIRST ONE."

WHAT I LOVED ABOUT TODAY:

"YOU CANNOT STOP THE WAVES, BUT YOU CAN LEARN TO SURF."

DATE : ....

WHAT I LOVED ABOUT TODAY:

"IT'S NOT ABOUT WHAT YOU'VE DONE. IT'S ABOUT WHAT YOU'RE DOING. IT'S ALL ABOUT WHERE YOU'RE GOING, NO MATTER WHERE YOU'VE BEEN."

DATE : ....

WHAT I LOVED ABOUT TODAY:

"LIFE IS LONG. THERE WILL BE PAIN BUT LIFE GOES ON WITH EVERYDAY A BRAND NEW SONG."

DATE : ....

WHAT I LOVED ABOUT TODAY:

"A JOURNEY OF A THOUSAND MILES BEGINS
WITH A SINGLE STEP."

WHAT I LOVED ABOUT TODAY:

"WHY HAVE REGRETS? EVERYTHING THAT'S GOING TO HAPPEN TO YOU IS GOING TO HAPPEN."

DATE : ....

WHAT I LOVED ABOUT TODAY:

"LET YOUR LIGHT SHINE. BE A SOURCE OF STRENGTH AND COURAGE. SHARE YOUR WISDOM. RADIATE LOVE."

DATE : ....

WHAT I LOVED ABOUT TODAY:

"WHEN YOU TRY AND CONTROL EVERYTHING, YOU ENJOY NOTHING. RELAX, BREATHE, LET GO AND LIVE."

DATE : ....

WHAT I LOVED ABOUT TODAY:

"YOU CAN RUN AWAY FROM YOUR PROBLEMS JUST
AS EASILY AS YOU CAN ESCAPE YOUR SHADOW."

WHAT I LOVED ABOUT TODAY:

"MILLIONS OF PEOPLE CAN BELIEVE IN YOU, YET NONE OF IT MATTERS UNLESS YOU BELIEVE IN YOURSELF."

DATE : ....

WHAT I LOVED ABOUT TODAY:

"WHEN LIFE GIVES YOU SOMETHING THAT MAKES YOU FEEL AFRAID, THAT'S WHEN LIFE GIVES YOU A CHANCE TO GROW STRONG AND BE BRAVE."

WHAT I LOVED ABOUT TODAY:

"WHEN SOMEONE ELSE'S HAPPINESS IS YOUR HAPPINESS, THAT IS LOVE."

DATE : ....

WHAT I LOVED ABOUT TODAY:

"ACCEPT WHAT YOU CAN'T CHANGE, AND
CHANGE WHAT YOU CAN'T ACCEPT."

WHAT I LOVED ABOUT TODAY:

"EVERYTHING YOU'VE EVER WANTED IS ON THE OTHER SIDE OF FEAR."

DATE : ....

WHAT I LOVED ABOUT TODAY:

"ANYONE CAN BE COOL, BUT AWESOME TAKES PRACTICE."

WHAT I LOVED ABOUT TODAY:

"THE VERY BEST MOTIVATION IS YOURSELF."

DATE : ....

WHAT I LOVED ABOUT TODAY:

"IF EVERYONE PRACTICED BEING WHO THEY ARE INSTEAD OF PRETENDING TO BE WHO THEY AREN'T, THERE WOULD BE PEACE."

WHAT I LOVED ABOUT TODAY:

"EVERYTHING HAPPENS FOR A REASON. MAYBE YOU DON'T SEE THE REASON RIGHT NOW, BUT WHEN IT IS FINALLY REVEALED IT WILL BLOW YOU AWAY."

DATE : ....

WHAT I LOVED ABOUT TODAY:

"IF YOU DON'T CUT A CAKE, IT'S ONLY ONE SLICE."

WHAT I LOVED ABOUT TODAY:

"CREATIVITY IS INTELLIGENCE HAVING FUN."

DATE : ....

WHAT I LOVED ABOUT TODAY:

"NOT EVERYTHING IN LIFE COMES IN HANDY, SO DON'T EXPECT TO GET EVERYTHING EASILY."

WHAT I LOVED ABOUT TODAY:

"IF WE DON'T KNOW OUR OWN WORTH, THEN WE SHOULDN'T EXPECT SOMEONE TO CALCULATE IT FOR US."

DATE : ....

WHAT I LOVED ABOUT TODAY:

"LOVE DOESN'T HURT, EXPECTATIONS DO."

DATE : ....

WHAT I LOVED ABOUT TODAY:

"LIFE IS TOO SHORT TO WORRY ABOUT STUPID THINGS.
HAVE FUN. FALL IN LOVE. REGRET NOTHING, AND DON'T
LET PEOPLE BRING YOU DOWN."

DATE : ....

WHAT I LOVED ABOUT TODAY:

"SOMETIMES I PRETEND TO BE NORMAL, BUT IT
GETS BORING. SO I GO BACK TO BEING ME."

DATE : ....

WHAT I LOVED ABOUT TODAY:

"PEOPLE ONLY RAIN ON YOUR PARADE BECAUSE THEY'RE JEALOUS OF YOUR SUN AND TIRED OF THEIR SHADE."

DATE : ....

WHAT I LOVED ABOUT TODAY:

"BE STRONG ENOUGH TO LET GO AND WISE ENOUGH TO
WAIT FOR WHAT YOU REALLY DESERVE."

DATE : ....

WHAT I LOVED ABOUT TODAY:

"SOMETIMES THE PEOPLE WITH THE BEST ADVICE ARE
THE ONES WITH THE MOST PROBLEMS."

DATE : ....

WHAT I LOVED ABOUT TODAY:

"IF YOU DON'T KNOW WHAT DIRECTION YOU'RE GOING,
HOW WILL YOU KNOW WHEN YOU GO OFF COURSE?"

DATE : ....

WHAT I LOVED ABOUT TODAY:

> "AS WE GROW OLDER, WE REALIZE WHAT WE
> NEED TO LEAVE BEHIND.'

DATE : ....

WHAT I LOVED ABOUT TODAY:

"YOU WILL NEVER GET WHAT YOU TRULY DESERVE IF YOU REMAIN ATTACHED TO WHAT YOU'RE SUPPOSED TO LET GO OF."

WHAT I LOVED ABOUT TODAY:

"THE KEY IS TO KEEP COMPANY ONLY WITH PEOPLE WHO UPLIFT YOU, WHOSE PRESENCE CALLS FORTH YOUR BEST."

DATE : ....

WHAT I LOVED ABOUT TODAY:

"BREAK THE RULES, STAND APART. IGNORE YOUR HEAD, FOLLOW YOUR HEART."

WHAT I LOVED ABOUT TODAY:

"VISUALIZE YOUR VICTORY."

DATE : ....

WHAT I LOVED ABOUT TODAY:

"WHEN YOU'RE HAPPY YOU ENJOY THE MUSIC, WHEN YOU'RE SAD YOU UNDERSTAND THE LYRICS."

DATE :

WHAT I LOVED ABOUT TODAY:

"LIFE IS A PURE FLAME, AND WE LIVE BY AN
INVISIBLE SUN WITHIN US."

353

DATE : ....

WHAT I LOVED ABOUT TODAY:

"VERY LITTLE IS NEEDED TO MAKE A HAPPY LIFE: IT IS ALL WITHIN YOURSELF, IN YOUR WAY OF THINKING."

WHAT I LOVED ABOUT TODAY:

"BY BEING YOURSELF, YOU PUT SOMETHING WONDERFUL IN THE WORLD THAT WASN'T THERE BEFORE."

DATE : ....

WHAT I LOVED ABOUT TODAY:

"BE SO HAPPY THAT WHEN OTHERS LOOK AT YOU THEY BECOME HAPPY TOO."

WHAT I LOVED ABOUT TODAY:

"HOLD THE VISION, TRUST THE PROCESS."

DATE : ....

WHAT I LOVED ABOUT TODAY:

"DON'T LIMIT YOURSELF TO THE SKIES WHEN THERE IS A WHOLE GALAXY OUT THERE."

WHAT I LOVED ABOUT TODAY:

"STAY POSITIVE AND THE UPS WILL BE MORE FREQUENT THAN THE DOWNS."

DATE : ....

WHAT I LOVED ABOUT TODAY:

"FOLLOW YOUR DREAMS. THEY KNOW THE WAY."

WHAT I LOVED ABOUT TODAY:

"THINK HAPPY THOUGHTS AND PUT A SMILE ON YOUR FACE SO THAT POSITIVE OPPORTUNITIES CAN FIND YOU."

DATE : ....

WHAT I LOVED ABOUT TODAY:

"THE GREATEST WEAPON AGAINST STRESS IS THE ABILITY TO CHOOSE ONE THOUGHT OVER ANOTHER."

WHAT I LOVED ABOUT TODAY:

"PEOPLE CHANGE AND OFTEN, THEY BECOME THE PERSON THEY SAID THEY WILL NEVER BE."

DATE : ....

WHAT I LOVED ABOUT TODAY:

"THINK OF ALL THE BEAUTY STILL LEFT AROUND YOU, AND BE HAPPY."

WHAT I LOVED ABOUT TODAY:

"YOU ONLY LIVE ONCE, SO THINK TWICE."

DATE : ....

WHAT I LOVED ABOUT TODAY:

"ALL MY LIFE I HAVE TRIED TO PLUCK A THISTLE AND PLANT A FLOWER WHEREVER THE FLOWER WOULD GROW IN THOUGHT AND MIND."

WHAT I LOVED ABOUT TODAY:

"EVERYTHING IN YOUR LIFE IS A REFLECTION OF A CHOICE YOU HAVE MADE. IF YOU WANT A DIFFERENT RESULT, MAKE A DIFFERENT CHOICE."

DATE : ....

WHAT I LOVED ABOUT TODAY:

"IF YOU CAN'T BE A PENCIL TO WRITE ANYONE'S HAPPINESS, THEN TRY TO BE AN ERASER TO REMOVE SOMEONE'S SADNESS."

DATE : ....

WHAT I LOVED ABOUT TODAY:

"NO MATTER HOW GOOD OR BAD YOU THINK LIFE IS,
WAKE UP EACH DAY AND BE THANKFUL FOR LIFE.
SOMEONE SOMEWHERE IS FIGHTING TO SURVIVE."

DATE : ....

WHAT I LOVED ABOUT TODAY:

"IF YOU HAVE GOOD THOUGHTS THEY WILL
SHINE OUT OF YOUR FACE LIKE SUNBEAMS AND
YOU WILL ALWAYS LOOK LOVELY."

WHAT I LOVED ABOUT TODAY:

"YOU ARE ALLOWED TO BE BOTH A MASTERPIECE AND A WORK IN PROGRESS SIMULTANEOUSLY."

Made in the USA
Lexington, KY
22 December 2017